Natta BEE

Not a MODEL.
How to stop feeling ugly.
Tips By A Non-Psychologist.

Natta Bee. How to stop feeling ugly

The Imperfect One

The alarm clock rang so abruptly that I jumped on the bed, and my heart pounded in my chest, ready to jump out. I don't want to get up! The gray sky outside the window only increased my desire to stay in bed. But in order to be able to succumb to this desire, one would have to be born into the family of some billionaire, where a whole staff of servants is a common thing. And those who have not been lucky enough to be the offspring of a rich family, or, at worst, to marry a rich guy, have to grit their teeth and go face the new day, in which you will encounter the not-very-exciting, routine-filled life of a simple employee.

I slowly sat up and barely opened my eyes. The reflection in the mirror on the wall only made the bad mood worse. But why? Why do some people have a luxurious full mane, instead of thin hair sticking out in different directions, not reacting to the ton of masks and balms with which I spoil it daily? Why do some people have a clear smooth skin, not covered with freckles, blemishes and redness? Why do some people have big eyes of the purest blue color? Why was I away when God handed out beauty to everyone, and I got stuck with the leftovers?

For me, as for most ordinary women, looks have always been a stumbling block. I was never satisfied with myself, and it always seemed to me that the people around me were much prettier. And even the assurances of friends and acquaintances that I was 'not bad at all' could not change my view of my own ugliness.

The opinion of others clashed with the ideal of a woman that I had created, that I had to be. It lived in my head all my life, from the very moment I began to understand what 'beautiful' and 'ugly' meant. Beautiful - when you have long, slim legs, thin waist and large breasts. Ugly - when the legs are of medium length, without the desired thigh gap, when the waist does not fit into the established 90-60-90 measurements, and the breasts don't even go beyond an A cup. Beautiful – when you have big eyes, full lips, perfectly smooth, velvety skin, and long, thick eyelashes. Otherwise – ugly.

But how can you live if all that nature has given you fits under your own description of 'ugly'? Is it possible to come to terms with this? Every time you stand in front of a mirror, you don't see anything like the astonishing beauty you have in your dreams, but instead something that is completely ordinary, imperfect, not noticeable at all. And the crying shame is that you will never become such a beauty, try as you might – you can't argue with nature and genes. You can, of course, try your luck and surrender to the mercy of a plastic surgeon, but, as practice shows, the result is not always as expected. And not everyone can afford such treat. And, besides, how much would you need to change to become like your dreams? Sure, you'll correct your face, but what about your legs and waist? In general, that's not what I would ever choose, especially since I'm fainting from just seeing a syringe in the treatment room, but here you would need to voluntarily go under the knife.

That's how you live from day to day with a sense of your own defectiveness. You pass by bright banners with perfect long-legged beauties and you usually think 'But why?'.

Or glance in the glossy magazine, and from there unearthly creatures look at you with a thin waist and large breasts, just like you'd always wanted. And again a cry is bursting out of my chest 'But why?'. How unjust this word is! Someone gets legs and eyes and hair, and someone else gets none of it.

Irritated, I turned away from the mirror and got up. This imperfect one needed to freshen herself up and go to work.

The bus was completely packed, the people from the back were pressing forward and I had to almost lie against the elderly gentleman standing in front of me, in an old-fashioned wide brim hat. At first he courageously withstood the pressure from me and a dozen other passengers, but then he couldn't take it anymore and turned around.

'I'm sorry' – I shyly muttered, while trying to stand on my own feet. But then the bus veered sharply, and I again fell against the old man in a hat.

'Never mind,' he chuckled, 'everything is allowed to such a beautiful young lady.'

'You are flattering me,' I objected, and before my mind's eye appeared the ideal woman, the one with which I could not compare.

'Of course, beautiful,' the old man smiled. 'And what you, young lady, have in your head - it's nothing but your own fantasies. Kick them out of that head of yours and live happily.'

He got off after a few stops, smiling at me for the last time - and I could not get his words out of my head. My fantasies? Kick my 'ideal woman' out of my head? Is that even possible? But maybe I should try after all, and then maybe I could 'live happily' after that, just like this random fellow traveler advised me?

Whose fault is it?

Most women, like me, have their own idea about how they look. And very often this idea is far from reality. Only few people think that their appearance is ideal, and millions of clients of plastic surgery clinics prove again and again that those of the fairer sex are ready to actively fight their own imperfections. At the same time, the streets are full of hundreds of truly beautiful women, who, unlike you, nature has generously endowed with all that is necessary. How surprised would you be if, asking any one of them, you'd get an honest answer – that they also consider themselves ugly. Unbelievable! No image of themselves in the mirror, no assurances from others, not even the endless compliments from men can fix this situation. Why? What is the problem?

It's simple - the reasons for such categorical self-rejection should be sought from the inside, not the outside.

Yes, within yourself. It's exactly where the idea 'I'm ugly' has taken root and has been living for many years. Where did it come from? Maybe someone deliberately put it in the female brain so that we couldn't be comfortable anywhere, and so we'd have to live with a feeling of inferiority all our lives? Indeed, the birth of this idea was to some extent because of the others. But only a little. For the rest, the woman herself contributes to the fact that this belief grows stronger from year to year. She constantly searches for dozens of proofs of her own imperfection, infinitely repeats them in her head, programming herself to believe that she is really an ugly creature. And the reflection in the mirror confirms it every time. That's how our brain is made - we notice only what our attention is drawn to. If you are concerned about your not very straight legs, then you will always notice them first. If you are unhappy with your complexion, have no doubt: the only thing that you will notice in the mirror will be uneven skin, covered with freckles and spots. And on and on it goes.

Imperfections, imperfections, all around just imperfections. To fix them, even a lifetime wouldn't be enough. And that's why those of the fairer sex seek to part quickly with what doesn't satisfy them. But, since they are not fighting with their real image, but with an imaginary self, the result is often shocking. Who among us hasn't encountered the victims of such a 'remake', where a girl who was very sweet, in our opinion, has turned into a real monster, with lips swollen like dumplings, pumped-up cheekbones and eyebrows the size of half her face. Surely you've wondered 'Why did she do this to herself? This is real ugliness!'. But has this owner of immense lips and enormous eyebrows become happier? Very doubtful. After all, after some time, she will again find in herself something that requires a remake. Breasts, for example. As a rule, it is a serious problem for all women striving for an ideal. One gets the feeling that to be beautiful without a C-cup breast size is simply unrealistic. There are also those who are willing to increase this part of the female body to such a size that it's even scary to talk about it out loud. Will the bigger breasts become a guarantee of self-confidence? Not necessarily. Look at the hundreds of women and girls with enormous breasts, exposing their photos on the Internet. I'm thinking the same question: 'Why?'.

Why turn yourself into a freak - which certainly attracts everyone's attention, but isn't likely to deserve general admiration?

We have all been nagged for a long time with the words that each woman has her own special something, and ugly women don't exist. Those who manage to find themselves without drowning in their own insecurities are lucky. Such women, however imperfect they are, are always perceived by others as indisputably beautiful. I wish we, hundreds of thousands of ordinary women, could learn to love ourselves as nature created us.

We shouldn't try to deal with the imperfections that exist only in our heads. There is no harder work than working on yourself, but this is what you should do here and now, if you don't want to suffer all your life from your own ugliness. A little effort and life will change. And the first thing that should be learned on the way to a new life is: we are all different.

The most stupid thing that you could spend your life on is trying to fit yourself into a common standard.

Where did it come from? Who said that I should be of such height and such weight, and that my measurements must necessarily fit into the established 90-60-90? Where is that factory where the parts for ideal women are made, where they make supermodels who correspond to the established standard parameters out of them? All this is the fruit of human imagination, nothing more.

At one point, someone decided that only a woman with a particular set of traits can be considered beautiful. Why he decided that is not so important – rather, it's important that now we are suffering and trying to at least somehow fit in, getting neuroses in pursuit of an impossible dream. Well, think for yourself: if your mom and dad endowed you with short height and a wide frame, will you be able to ever reach such necessary measurements? Of course not. And it's not necessary after all. Such a senseless chasing after some mythical ideal will never make you a beautiful woman - that's for sure. To become such a woman, you need to find the root of the problem and eliminate it. Let's try to understand yourself and, if possible, get rid of everything that prevents a woman from revealing her attractiveness. Give it a try! A new self!

Returning to childhood

Childhood is an amazing time, when the whole world is smiling at us. Remember, when else in your life have you had so many positive emotions as in childhood? Every day new discoveries awaited us, making us look at the world with eyes wide open. A small child is the center of any family, and a little girl is definitely a princess. Fancy dresses, funny pigtails, large bows - these are of course all the traits of a real princess.

Each of us remembers how happy she was about her new outfit and how she was swirling around in front of the mirror, considering herself the most beautiful in the world. Stop right there. That's it, this feeling, in the moment when you don't doubt your own irresistibility. We have all experienced it. Where did it disappear, and why is it that now, many years later, instead of 'I'm the most beautiful', we think 'I'm just ugly', or something like that? When did the program get corrupted, and who made it happen?

Children are pure creatures, open to everything that brings them joy. And, since they don't have their own experience yet, they very quickly absorb the experience of others and other people's opinions, taking them as the ultimate truth.

11

Of course, the most important is the opinion of their parents. Growing up, a child goes to kindergarten and then to school, and there they encounter the opinions of other adults and peers. And the more a person means to them, the more important his opinion will be.

But let's go back to those happy days, when the baby had the closest people – mom and dad – right next to it. Of course, they wish us only good, and in their own way strive to ensure that our future life will be happy. Unfortunately, not all of them are armed with the diploma of a psychologist, so their actions are not always correct from the point of view of the development of a harmonious person, especially a woman who is confident of her own appeal. Very often, noticing that the daughter is about to turn into a real beauty, her mother deliberately undermines her self-esteem, devaluing or simply not noticing her visual appeal. After all, why raise an arrogant princess? It will be very hard afterwards for her, in adulthood.

There is a grain of truth to this - but, as practice shows, the majority of girls who heard criticisms from their relatives in childhood suffer from an inferiority complex in their adult life. And it's very difficult to get rid of it. It is not necessary that criticism flows from the lips of loved ones at all times. It's enough to hear just a few times the casual words: 'My chubby little angel!' or 'What a bottom you have there!', so that for the rest of your life you would see yourself as a fat cow with a huge posterior. A little girl cannot resist the opinion of the most important people in her world, and takes it as the very truth. Therefore, I would like to advise the parents of little princesses to be very cautious in their assessments. It is not necessary to embellish the advantages given by nature, but the existing ones should be noticed, so when the girl becomes a grown up woman she would be aware of her strengths.

But what about us, the women who heard in their childhood from their loved ones that they were not good enough? Maybe it happened at the age of three, or maybe when you were older. But in any case, such words could not remain unnoticed. Perhaps it was even that Mom or Dad didn't say anything in front of you, but they discussed your imperfections amongst themselves, and you accidentally overheard their conversation. It was exactly then that an idea that there is something wrong with you took root in your head. Now, looking at your reflection, you will begin to search for the same flaw that you heard them talking about. And maybe not only one. The girl grows, and with her the seed that her parents accidentally planted grows as well. As she gains more experience, the woman finds more and more confirmation of what she heard that one time. And it is very difficult for her to give up something that she was already convinced about in her childhood.

Changing the programming

What to do? Is there really no way to correct this situation? Nothing is impossible if you have firmly decided to understand your childhood programming. To do so, you need to take a small trip back in time. Yes, don't be surprised. It is necessary to return to childhood and discover the moment when you first heard unpleasant words from your loved ones. How to do it? There are many ways to reach your subconscious, where all the information collected during life is stored. Some people prefer to consult specialists for this. I managed to deal with it on my own.

It is better to choose a time when no one will bother you. Comfortably sitting in a chair or on a bed, close your eyes and imagine yourself as a little girl. Relive the brightest moments of your childhood. It's possible that you won't be able to discover the words you're looking for the first time. But don't stop searching. Over time, you will remember how and what your mother said that was the starting point in your struggle with yourself. Some women remember this moment so clearly that they don't need to go back in time to search for it. But despite this, they still haven't understood what to do with this knowledge.

Now that you know exactly which belief is rooted in you from childhood, do a simple thing - release it from your head.

Tell yourself (you can do it aloud): 'This is just an opinion that has nothing to do with reality'. You grew up and realized that your mother was wrong. Remind yourself that she is an ordinary person, not God. Now, every time you try to discover in yourself the imperfection your mother pointed to, repeat: 'This is just the opinion of one person, which does not affect the true image of the world in any way' (you can think of something simpler too). Over time, you will cease to perceive according to your childhood programming, and will be able to see yourself as you really are.

Another way to deal with childhood programming is to replace a negative parental affirmation with your own positive one.

For example, if you found out that it was your mother who made you believe that your legs were ugly, then, every time when an idea about crooked legs comes in your mind, repeat that they are wonderful. This may sound silly, but the method really works. Nothing contributes to the formation of our own particular reality as much as the multiple repetition of an affirmation. Why not use this method to improve your self-esteem?

How does the environment affect you?

Even if during your childhood your loved ones didn't plant a time bomb in your head called 'something is wrong with my appearance', don't worry - there will always be those who try to put this idea in you head.

People tend to see imperfections in others, and, most importantly, they point to these imperfections even when they are not asked to do it.

Perhaps such an approach makes sense in the case of performing some professional duties, which will force the employee to do everything possible to improve their performance. But what's the point of criticizing someone's appearance? And in the open, telling it to their faces? It's not like after your harsh remarks, the owner of a small bust or a long nose will immediately get rid of it.

Another reason for our discontent with our own appearance, in addition to what was put in our heads since childhood, is often the environment around us. Among your many friends and acquaintances there are always people ready to point out a thousand and one imperfections that you have, which do not allow you to come closer to your ideal. Here you should remember that the opinion of these 'brave defenders of truth' is as subjective as the opinion of your loved ones who once, long ago, managed to shake your calm natural harmony. Still, the words of a close friend or a good acquaintance can be very painful. And, listening to such remarks regularly, it is not difficult to develop strong complexes.

I used to have a friend - let's call her M. Every time she saw me wearing a new dress or pretty bow, M would say 'It doesn't fit you'. At the same time, she looked at me with pure, naive eyes, in which the only desire was to help her friend not to look worse than the others. I felt awfully ugly, having put on such inappropriate attire. For many years I continued to be friends with this girl, not realizing that it was her who caused my constant insecurity at all school events, and, indeed, in everyday life as well. Needless to say, if there was a good looking classmate next to me and I was glowing from his attention, my friend would immediately bring me crashing down to earth, by her very presence reminding me of how ugly I was. Who knows how my life would have turned out if I had continued to communicate with this person? Fortunately, our paths split after graduation, and little by little communication fell away as well.

On the path of life, I also met other people who wanted to influence my perception of myself. However, I was now much older, and was already not going to surrender to someone else's opinion - although, given the already negative attitude towards my own appearance, I very often found confirmation of it in the words of those 'well-wishers'. 'But they are right,' I thought, looking in the mirror, 'my legs are chubby, and my nose is somehow crooked.' Such 'compliments' rain down on each of us as from an unending spring. You can agree with me that hearing kind words from your co-workers, friends or just acquaintances is much more difficult than hearing criticism. Especially those who simply envy you are trying the most in this regard.

Most women in everyday life are constantly faced with criticism of their own appearance.

And without realizing it, they get a new burden added to their already existing complexes. Our brains readily accept what ears regularly hear, and so the opinion of your co-worker becomes your personal opinion. Remember: after the words thrown at you during lunch break by the lovely-looking woman from the office, your appearance has not changed, only your attitude towards yourself has changed.

I am even more outraged by men who believe that they have the right to criticize the appearance of their girlfriend and to alter it as they want. Unfortunately, under the influence of feelings for their beloved man, women are ready to do everything: change, give themselves up and become one of the average beauties. I'm not a psychologist, and I cannot claim for sure, but it seems that this is done by those of the fairer sex who are already suffering from disliking themselves. Otherwise, why change myself, if everything in me is beautiful already?

Choosing the best

The advice in this situation is obvious: change the environment. There's no point in waiting for the time when, thanks to the continued efforts of others, your small complexes will become a real problem. No matter how hard it is to give up an old friend or a loved one, you need to stop communicating with them. At least until you realize what negativity comes from them, and until you stop taking criticism as truth.

That's exactly what I did in the case of my school friend M. At first, I missed her, but then I began to notice that without this person I felt much better. I stopped being afraid of not meeting the expectations of another person. Now I don't worry that a new dress doesn't fit me, or that my makeup is too provocative. Looking at my reflection in the mirror, I began to notice that there are as many good things in me as flaws. My man helped me to strengthen this thought, never getting tired of telling me over and over how beautiful I was.

Now I know for sure: in order to feel like a beautiful woman, you shouldn't listen to those who are examining your imperfections under a magnifying glass.

You should surround yourself with people who regularly remind you of your attractiveness.

Very soon you will feel like a completely different person! Nobody has ever disproven the saying that the woman loves with her ears. That's how we are made - we need to HEAR how beautiful we are. Only then does a woman truly blossom.

And one more little advice. If you don't have people around you who regularly praise you, do it yourself. Call it what you want: 'affirmations', 'self-help', etc. - the main thing is to give yourself compliments. You can do this while standing in front of a mirror, sitting in public transport, walking, or doing household chores. I confirmed it on myself: the statement 'I'm very pretty', repeated several times a day, increases your appeal in your own eyes by 50%. You can talk about yourself in general, or examine each of your qualities separately: for example your luxurious hair, or your slim legs. Your brain will gladly 'swallow' the bait, and after a while the first results will appear. You will begin to notice in yourself not imperfections, but strengths - and this is the direct path towards feeling like a beautiful woman.

About stereotypes

Have you noticed that, after looking through glossy magazines, your mood is often ruined? Your positive feelings drop to zero. For a long time I could not understand why. After all, these publications are designed so that we, the average women, can come into contact with the beautiful side of life. On the smooth pages made from expensive paper you can find the latest innovations in the cosmetics industry, luxury clothes, expensive cars and posh women. Stop – that's it.

Posh women in glossy magazines - that's what lowers my self-esteem. They are so beautiful that it is very difficult to get over it for an ordinary, imperfect representative of the fairer sex.

For a long time I continued to buy magazines with maniacal regularity and be green with envy about the beauties on the front page, until I realized that this was the worst thing I could do to myself. I would never become so fancy, so why reopen the wound each time? And I made the only right decision - I stopped spending money on something that makes me unhappy. Already after a week of this voluntary refusal of printed beauty, I felt much better. Having stopped constantly comparing myself with unreal beauties, I started to pay less attention to my own imperfections. Magazines disappeared from my life forever.

However, it was not so easy to solve the problem. Each time I went into the street, or in a large shopping mall, I ran the risk of encountering other beauties - on large advertisement billboards and banners. And they were not inferior to the beauties in the magazines - they were the same: long-legged, big-breasted and big-eyed. How can one not get upset? They were looking at me with contemptuous smiles, as if hinting that I would never get to be on such a banner myself. Do I even need to say that all my negative thoughts about my own imperfections once again made a space for themselves in my head?

Television broadcasts and advertising only added fuel to the fire. Every evening, breathtakingly fancy women looked at me arrogantly from the television screen, and I realized that it would be easier to drink poison than to get even a little closer to these heavenly creatures. I did not get rid of the TV - it's expensive, and my family would not approve. It's possible, of course, to give it up just like I gave up magazines. But apart from the fancy women on TV, they also show some very useful programs. What to do then?

It was necessary to solve this problem urgently, and an idea came in my head. First of all, it was necessary to understand why I reacted with such pain to girls on TV or in a glossy magazine. The answer was obvious - I consciously thought they were more beautiful. But if we dig deeper, this was not my own opinion, but the stereotype imposed on me. Isn't it true? Just as in my childhood I was told about imperfections unknown to me, or had them persistently imposed on me in adulthood, I was now being asked to comply with the prevailing standard. This is nothing but a manipulation of consciousness, with which a big part of those of the fairer sex are complacent. You can go with the flow and try to match the unreal ideal without much success, or accept yourself as you are, no matter how trivial this may sound.

How to create your own stereotype?

To fight stereotypes is rather difficult. The image created on the screen or in the magazine is considered as a universally recognized ideal of beauty and a reference standard, to which all women should resemble, regardless of their genetic characteristics, complexion, etc. Sometimes this fight is not for life, but for death, and we know dozens of sad stories with unhappy endings, where women sacrificed their health and life in order to become like those who are all over the advertisements and TV. Striving to be 'like you're supposed to be' is the most hopeless task.

The standards of beauty have been changing throughout the long history of mankind.

In the Middle Ages women with flat breasts were valued, and this part of the female body was pulled together by corsets. Then the fashion for curvier bodies arrived, and ladies began to use small pieces of padding to correspond to the ideal. A little more time passed, and on the pedestal rose girls with a boyish figure, etc. Today one type is in style, tomorrow there will be another, and no woman can keep up with the changing fashions.

Is it possible to not be guided by stereotypes? It is possible, of course. Why not come up with your own ideal of beauty? The kind that your particular traits fit perfectly. Let, for example, short women with medium complexion and 95-76-105 measurements be most valued in your Universe. Who could stop you from doing this? Today, the opinion that each person forms their own reality is more and more widespread. I suggest starting with forming your own stereotype about female beauty. Of course, this does not mean that a woman should not strive for perfection, but rather only to extent that this is possible according to the qualities that nature has given her. Only after cautiously evaluating our own characteristics we can create an ideal for ourselves and strive for it without the danger of harming ourselves.

Moreover, you can change your standard of beauty over time. And it will be a good standard, given that we change under the influence of age and circumstances.

The advantages of such a 'flexible standard' are obvious. It takes into account the individuality of each of us and does not require us to get in over our heads. I admit that I have already changed my standard several times, each time writing down 'ideal' measurements in my special notebook. I can say with certainty that many recognized beauties are not at all beautiful according to the rules of my world. And this idea warms me up every time I walk past the next advertising banner or watch TV.

The most important thing – don't be lazy!

Now that we've figured out the main psychological factors that make women feel ugly, it's worth thinking about how to improve ourselves. Above I mentioned that this should be done strictly in accordance with your own standards of beauty. Perhaps some of the fairer sex are quite comfortable in their current shape. But I believe that most of us strive to improve our appearance as much as possible.

In my opinion, the best way to maintain beauty and achieve perfect shape is physical exercise.

And this is the first thing you should do if you think your body is imperfect. Exercise makes us not only beautiful, but also healthy, and the trained body looks much more attractive than the one that has never experienced physical exercise. I'm glad that today it's fashionable to be fit. This allows you to add points to your own attractiveness.

I am opposed to torturing oneself for hours at the fitness club. From sports, as well as from any other activity, you should be getting pleasure. Only then it will be beneficial. Because we are all different, the level of our physical abilities also differs. Someone perhaps prefers morning runs in the park and cannot tolerate exercises using gym equipment. I, for instance, hate running. That's simply not my thing. It's easier for me to go to a group workout than circle around on a running path.

I used to follow strictly the recommendations of specialists, and if they said that running was the best way to lose weight, I would force myself to run in the morning. Needless to say, the pleasure I got from such activities was close to zero. Today, my motto is as follows:

Do what gives you pleasure, but do it well - and the result will not disappoint you.

Can't run – then walk; don't want to lift heavy stuff in the gym – then do yoga or stretching. Whatever we do for our bodies will certainly repay us back. And vice versa – if we stop paying attention to ourselves, then very soon we will become enormous fatties with sagging skin. I haven't met a single woman who would still remain attractive without putting any effort in it.

The same can be said about facial care. As advised by cosmetologists, you should start no later than at the age of twenty-five, although minimal skin care is necessary for even very young girls. Over time, you will have to put more and more effort into remaining young and beautiful. Nowadays there are excellent techniques that allow you to take some ten years off your age. And this doesn't need to include plastic surgery. Any cosmetologist is ready to offer to the representatives of the fairer sex dozens of effective procedures for personal care, in various price ranges. You don't need to be a millionaire's wife to treat yourself at least a few times a year. But what to do if there is no money for a cosmetologist at the moment? No money at all? Continue to do what is possible at home. Peelings, creams, masks – that's the only way.

I have a friend who in her youth was a real beauty: the right facial features, luxurious hair, a slim figure. All the boys were crazy about her, and all the girls envied the generosity with which nature had spoiled her. We hadn't seen each other for about fifteen years, when, not long ago, someone called out my name on the street. I stared for a long time at a chubby woman with a sagging face that had never known even basic care. And suddenly I realized: 'It's N! How merciless time is! What it has made of this beautiful girl!'

I silently listened to her story about her children and husband, and repeated to myself that I would never become like her - I don't want to! The next day I spent two hours instead of one hour at the gym, and in the evening I put on a rejuvenating mask with collagen. Perhaps each of us needs to have such an example, confirming that, if we don't work on ourselves, even the most beautiful girls eventually turn into scary old women. Are you ready to become one of those? In my case, absolutely not. I will do everything in order to still look young and beautiful when I die.

I would like to remind many women about the role of decorative cosmetics. I assure you, it was not created to take time away, but to subtly improve our appearance. I am against using a large quantity of make-up on the face, but powder, lipstick and mascara are necessary for everyone of the fairer sex. Unfortunately, the life of modern women is not usually conducive to a healthy blush of the cheeks. We sleep too little, we are nervous too often and we don't eat well. But is it necessary that all this should be visible in our faces? For whom is this important? For people around, it's much more pleasant to communicate with you if you have smooth skin, with the blue lines under the eyes hidden with the help of the corrector.

I am particularly amazed by those women who forego the help of decorative cosmetics after having celebrated their fortieth birthday.

At the age of twenty, a girl was using make-up so much that it was impossible to recognize her under all those layers, but at the age of forty she decides: enough of that, I'm so beautiful! Exactly when the age begins to show its signs and it would not hurt to hide them. I think it's stupid. Perhaps in the mirror you continue to see yourself as young and youthful, but others around you see a completely different picture.

I'm wondering, why do women stop taking care of themselves? Why are they getting fat, giving up cosmetics, not caring for their skin? What is the cause of that? Being too tired? To some extent it is that. But mostly, it's laziness. They stop doing it because they are too lazy to get up early to go for a run in the park, too lazy to spend 15 minutes on make-up, too lazy to put a mask on their face. Why? Because, they think, they should be loved the way they are. And at the same time only few women are happy with their appearance. But if you're not happy, you should do something to change it. If the imperfections are there on your face, you can even make yourself believe on a regular basis that you are a great beauty, but we know that it's not true. You cannot fool yourself.

It's way easier to give up on yourself and continue to look with envy at the photos of slim beauties in magazines. To change your life dramatically is much more difficult. That's why those women who have managed to turn from ugly ducklings into beautiful swans deserve more respect. One can only envy their willpower. By their example, they prove that nothing is impossible if you really want it.

How to stop feeling ugly?

There is a funny saying: 'There are no ugly women, there is just too little alcohol'. In fact, it's true that there are no ugly women: there are only women who are not confident in themselves and women who have given up on themselves. Often one is related to another. When a very attractive girl feels that she looks ugly from the point of view of others, it's a matter of complexes – but when a woman objectively does not create a good impression, that's laziness. Each of us is capable of changing this situation.

You do not need to be a great expert in psychology in order to reach the conclusion that beautiful women love themselves, they are satisfied with their appearance and they don't try to be like others. But there are not that many such representatives of the fairer sex. Even very attractive women from time to time have a feeling of insecurity. And often they get helped along towards this, as we mentioned above. Therefore, before stepping on the path towards improving yourself and your life, it is necessary to deal with your own internal 'bats in the belfry'. Let me remind you that a short guide for reaching the world of beauty and peace of mind consists of several important steps.

- Changing your childhood programming. If a negative attitude towards yourself was implanted in you since childhood, you should remove this programming from your subconscious. We adults

31

are capable of controlling our thoughts, aren't we? Why repeat to yourself every time what your mother said, when you can replace this statement with another, emphasizing your good qualities, not your flaws?

- Analyzing your environment and refusing to communicate with those who have a negative attitude. People who constantly criticize your appearance should be removed from your circle of close associates. Find yourself girlfriends and acquaintances who are ready to pay you compliments and support you. And then there will be dramatic changes in your perception of yourself.

- Refusing stereotypes. At the next stage, you will have to go into battle against the stereotypes of beauty that are imposed on us. Everyone decides on their own how to do it. I prefer to create my own measurements of an ideal woman, as I explained before. Each of us should have their own way of not falling for the bait of marketing specialists and other professionals who are trying to fit everyone into one mold.

In general, I am annoyed by the desire to make us a sort of herd, where everybody is like another. At such times you should tell yourself 'I'm not like everybody else', and step aside. Why should I turn my lips into swollen dumplings just because everyone does it? This is complete nonsense. I am me, and others are others.

In my childhood, when I would do something stupid, I would explain to my mother that 'everyone did that', and she always asked me: 'And if everyone jumps off the roof, will you jump as well?'. In my opinion, that's a great parallel.

If everyone 'jumps off the roof' by making extraordinary and often frightening changes to their appearance, I don't have to do what they did, do I?

- And, most importantly, you must CONSTANTLY work on yourself in order to feel beautiful. The more effort you put into your own beauty, the more you will appreciate it. So what if you weren't born so beautiful? Be sure to preserve the gift you were given, carry it with you throughout the years, exposed to the influence of age and life's adversities - and at the same time not lose it, so that you're no less beautiful on the day you die than when you were born.

Only few women can boast that they have become better with age. But this is quite possible. However, you will need to perform the necessary rituals every day to maintain your beauty, regardless of your mood or the weather outside your window. And here everything depends not on the advantages that nature has given you, but on your willpower and organization.

Then, many years later, you won't need to look sadly at your old photos, remembering 'how I used to look' - but you will be able to admire yourself in the present instead.

Every woman can be beautiful, or become beautiful, while preserving her own individuality - that special something that is so appreciated by those of the opposite sex. But this is not even about them. The main thing is that a beautiful woman makes the world around her beautiful, and makes her family and friends happy. She is confident in herself, loves herself and is ready to share this love. As the great Russian classic said: 'Beauty will save the world'. We are many, and all of us different, but this is the main point of nature itself.

See how varied our world is: it has a place for people both thin and fat, with white and black skin, blondes and brunettes. Together we create harmony, each one contributing something by themselves.

If suddenly all women became identical, the harmony would be broken. Therefore, it is so important in the pursuit of beauty to remain yourself. Do you want to be beautiful? Then be! Here and now. Everything depends only on you!

www.ingramcontent.com/pod-product-compliance
Lightning Source LLC
Chambersburg PA
CBHW072027280526
45788CB00007B/2699